# GETTING CREATIVE WITH
# WALLPAPER & PAINT

CREATIVE
PUBLISHING
international

CHANHASSEN, MINNESOTA
www.creativepub.com

*President / CEO*: Michael Eleftheriou
*Vice President / Publisher*: Linda Ball
*Vice President / Retail Sales*: Kevin Haas

GETTING CREATIVE WITH
WALLPAPER & PAINT

*Created by*: The Editors of Creative
Publishing international, Inc.

*Printed on American paper by*:
 R. R. Donnelley
10 9 8 7 6 5 4 3 2

Creative Publishing international, Inc.
offers a variety of how-to-books. For
information write:
     Creative Publishing international, Inc.
      Subscriber Books
     18705 Lake Drive East
     Chanhassen, MN 55317

GETTING CREATIVE WITH

# WALLPAPER & PAINT

# Contents

# Introduction

Creative wall treatments and unique accents applied to furniture and accessories are the personal touches that give your home its distinctive character. While a fresh coat of paint can alter a color scheme and entirely change the design dynamics in a room, the visual texture and depth created by special decorative painting techniques enhance the new look with elegance and flair. Decorative details created with wallcovering borders, cutouts, and panels establish interesting focal points in a room, taking advantage of the flawless patterns and rich colors of this readily available product.

Doing it yourself has never been easier or more affordable. With a rainbow of paint colors to choose from and a wide array of wallcovering products at your fingertips, you can turn every room in your home into a designer's dream. Painting techniques, like sponging, rag rolling, and texturizing, are not complicated; with a little practice on a sheet of tag board, you can move right into painting your walls. Paint glazes that you mix yourself allow you to work with the paint longer, giving you plenty of time to get just the look you want. By designing with wallcovering borders, cutouts, and panels, unique professional looks can be achieved at far less cost than it would take to paper the entire room. And all it takes is a little planning and a patient hand with a scissors or craft knife.

So don't put off those decorating plans any longer. *Getting Creative with Wallpaper & Paint* is your guide to giving your home the designer appearance you see in today's trendsetting magazines. You'll be amazed at how easy it can be.

# *Papering Projects*

Wallpaper has long been a recognized term used for the decorative covering applied to walls. Though in the past, these decorative coverings were indeed made of paper, today the broader term, wallcovering, is used to include other materials, such as vinyls and natural fibers.

Aside from papering entire walls, there are many creative uses for wallcoverings that can be accomplished in smaller projects. Wallcoverings can be incorporated into your decorating scheme to achieve a custom-designed look with professional results.

Wallcovering borders and cutouts can be applied in various ways to create interesting accents on walls. Isolated wallcovering panels break up expansive walls with decorative impact. Wallcovering borders make an effective chair rail or architectural accent.

Wallcovering can be applied to a cornice to create a custom-made window treatment. Motifs can be cut from wallpaper rolls or borders and applied to the flat surfaces of cabinets or furniture. Even lamp shades can be papered, adding pattern or texture to a room.

Easy techniques are explained with full-color photography, showing you countless ways to add creative touches with wallpaper.

# Wallcovering Basics

Wallcoverings may be used in many creative ways to add interest and variety to a decorating scheme. Wallcoverings with different patterns may be combined to achieve unique effects. To find wallcoverings that work well together, look for patterns that have similar colors or design motifs rather than limiting yourself to patterns that are designed as coordinates.

After selecting a wallcovering, consult the salesperson about the proper adhesive. Many wallcoverings are prepasted and do not need additional adhesive. The paste on these wallcoverings is activated by dipping the wallcovering in water. Unpasted wallcoverings are applied using a clear vinyl adhesive. Border adhesive is often recommended for applying a vinyl border over a vinyl wallcovering; any excess border adhesive must be removed immediately, because it is impossible to remove after it has dried. Some wallcovering pastes may discolor painted surfaces and touching up may be required.

Before applying a wallcovering, clean the wall surface to remove any grease or soil.

A solution of equal parts of ammonia and water works well. Repair any cracks or dents by filling them with spackling compound.

For some wallcovering applications, premixed sizing is recommended. This product prevents the adhesive from soaking into the wall surface. It also improves adhesion of the wallcovering and makes it easier to reposition, if necessary. Sizing is recommended for applications in humid areas. Once applied, sizing may be difficult to remove.

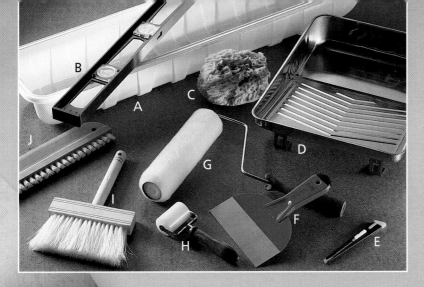

Tools required for papering projects include A. WATER TRAY for use with prepasted wallcovering, B. CARPENTER'S LEVEL, C. NATURAL SEA SPONGE, D. PAINT TRAY, E. RAZOR KNIFE with a breakaway blade, F. WIDE BROADKNIFE, G. PAINT ROLLER, H. SEAM ROLLER, I. PASTE BRUSH for applying adhesive to unpasted wallcovering, and J. SMOOTHING BRUSH.

# How to prepare wallcovering

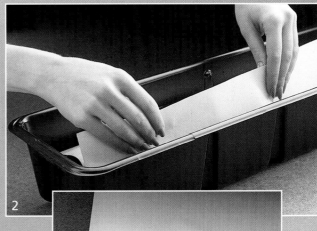

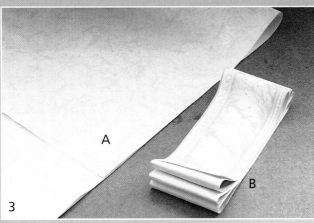

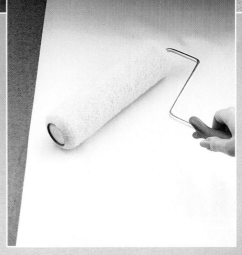

1. PREPASTED WALLCOVERING. Fill the water tray half full of lukewarm water. Roll the cut strip loosely, adhesive side out. Wet the roll in the tray as directed by the manufacturer, usually for about 1 minute or less.

2. Hold one edge of the strip with both hands, and lift the wallcovering from the water; check pasted side to make sure strip is evenly wet.

3. Cure short or vertical wallcovering strips by folding ends to center, pasted side in, without creasing folds (A); for long horizontal strips, fold the wallcovering strips accordion-style (B). Allow the strip to set for about ten minutes.

UNPASTED WALLCOVERING. Place the strip patterned side down on a flat surface. Apply adhesive evenly, using paint roller or paste brush. Wipe adhesive from table before preparing next strip. Cure strip as in step 3.

# WALL TREATMENTS

# Wallcovering Borders

Decorating with wallcovering borders is an easy way to add style to a room. Borders can be used to define a space, highlight architectural features, or add interest by creating new lines.

Available in a variety of designs, borders can be used to complement any decorating style. Designs include florals, geometrics, and architectural patterns. To achieve unique effects, borders can be cut apart or combined with other borders. For best results when using a border to outline or frame features of a room, select a border with a nondirectional print, because directional prints may not be pleasing when hung upside down. Some border designs are available with matching or coordinating corner pieces, which add a distinctive finishing touch. You can also make your own custom corner piece by cutting design motifs from wallcovering or wallcovering borders.

When determining the border placement, consider where the placement will draw the eye and what the placement will do to the proportions of the room. A border placed at the top of the wall draws the eye upward, providing a balance with elements at a lower level. Positioned at the picture rail level, a border visually lowers the ceiling. Consider running the border in a continuous band around doors and windows instead of ending the border when it meets the door and window moldings. For borders used as chair rails, position the center of the border one-third of the distance up from the floor on the wall surface.

When hanging borders, begin in an inconspicuous location. Plan the placement, if possible, so the more conspicuous corners are mitered evenly; corners at eye level or higher are usually more noticeable than lower corners. Where the last border segment meets the first, a mismatch usually results.

Wallcovering borders are available by the yard (m) or prepackaged in 5-yd. to 7-yd. (4.6 to 6.4 m) spools. To estimate the yardage needed, measure the areas where the border will be applied. Allow extra yardage for matching adjoining spools and for any damage that may have occurred to the ends of the rolls. Also allow at least twice the border width plus 2" (5 cm) for each mitered corner.

# How to hang wallcovering borders

1. Cut first border strip, and prepare strip (page 7). Draw a light pencil line around room at desired height, using a carpenter's level, if positioning the border at location other than ceiling or baseboard.

2. Position border at the least conspicuous corner. Overlap the border around corner of adjacent wall for 1/2" (1.3 cm). Press border flat along wall with a smoothing brush; have an assistant hold folded portion of border while you apply and brush it.

3. Form a 1/4" (6 mm) tuck just beyond each inside corner. Continue to apply border. Cut border at corner, using a sharp razor knife and wide broadknife.

**4.** Peel back the tucked strip, and smooth strip around the corner. Press the border flat. Apply seam adhesive to lapped seam, if necessary.

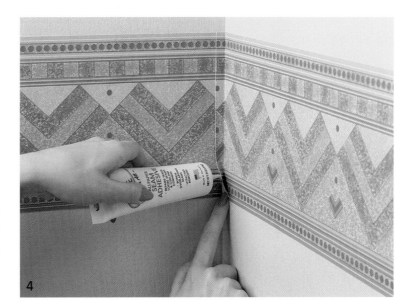

**5.** Overlap border strips so patterns match, if a seam falls in middle of wall. Cut through both layers, using a wide broadknife and a razor knife. Peel back border, and remove cut ends. Press border flat. Roll seam after ½ hour. Rinse adhesive from border, using damp sponge.

**6.** Trim border at a door or window frame by holding border against outer edge of frame with a wide broadknife and trimming excess with a sharp razor knife.

# How to miter wallcovering borders

1. Apply the horizontal border strips, extending them past the corners a distance greater than the width of the border. Apply the vertical border strips, overlapping the horizontal strips.

2. Cut through both layers at a 45° angle, using a razor knife and a straightedge. Peel back the border; remove ends.

3. Press the border flat. Roll the seam after 1/2 hour. Rinse adhesive from seam, using a damp sponge.

# TIPS FOR DECORATING WITH WALLCOVERING BORDERS

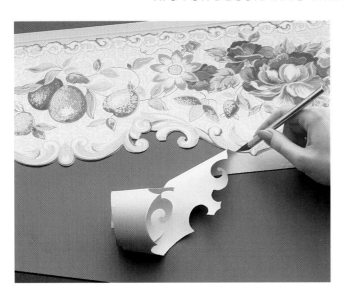

TRIM away upper or lower edges of the border along the lines of the design to create interesting effects.

MAKE borders economically by cutting standard rolls of wallcovering into border strips. Striped wallcoverings with nondirectional designs are especially suitable.

APPLY designs cut from borders over mitered corners to camouflage seams.

FINISH cut end of border with a strip of edging cut from additional length of border. Cut edging strip diagonally at corners to form a mitered appearance with edging on border.

# More ideas for wallcovering borders

OPPOSITE: DOUBLE ROW OF BOR-
DER STRIPS gives greater impact along
the ceiling.

RIGHT: DECORATIVE BORDER is positioned about 2 ft. (0.63 m) below the ceiling
to divide the wall.

BELOW: CEILING-LINE BORDER draws
the eye upward. The lower portion of the
border is cut away along the edge of the
design to integrate the border and the
painted wall.

*Continued*

# *More ideas for wallcovering borders*
## (CONTINUED)

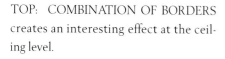

TOP: COMBINATION OF BORDERS creates an interesting effect at the ceiling level.

RIGHT: VERTICAL BORDER STRIPS can be used to divide plain walls. The placement guidelines were marked using a carpenter's level and pencil. An edging strip cut from an additional length of border is used to finish the upper and lower edges. The edging strips are applied to the cut ends of the border as on page 19.

ABOVE: MITERED BORDER frames a window. Design motifs from the border are cut out and applied over the miters to camouflage the seams (page 19).

# Wallcovering Panels

Wallcovering and coordinating borders can be used to create decorative wall panels. The panels are less costly than covering entire rooms and add interest to otherwise plain walls.

Make panels to divide large walls into smaller sections, or use panels to highlight pictures and mirrors. The panels may be identical in size, or wide panels may be alternated with narrow ones. As a general rule, space the panels evenly on the wall, allowing slightly more space between the lower edge of the panel and the baseboard. Begin by planning the placement of the most dominant panels first. You may want to plan placement on graph paper, taking into account the position of any windows, doors, or built-ins. Also take into account any pattern repeat in the wallcovering to allow for matching patterns, if necessary.

## How to make wallcovering panels

1. Determine the size and position of wallcovering panels by cutting and taping paper to the wall. Using a pencil and a carpenter's level, lightly mark the dimensions of the panel on the wall. Measure and record the dimensions.

2. Cut a strip of wallcovering for the center of the panel to size, using a framing square to ensure 90° angles at the corners. Prepare the wallcovering as on page 11.

3. Unfold the top portion of the prepared strip. Position lightly on the wall, aligning wallcovering with marked lines; use your palms to slide the strip in place. Press top of the strip flat with a smoothing brush, checking for bubbles, and reposition as necessary.

4

4. Unfold bottom of strip; use palms to position strip against marked lines. Press strip flat with smoothing brush, checking for bubbles.

5. Cut and apply any remaining strips, matching pattern and butting seams. Roll seam after 1/2 hour. Rinse any adhesive from the wallcovering and wall, using clear water and a damp sponge. Prepare border as for unpasted wallcovering (page 11), using border adhesive.

6. Apply border strips to panel in clockwise direction, starting at least conspicuous corner; align outer edge of border to edge of panel and allow ends to extend slightly beyond edges of panel. Miter corners as on page 18, steps 2 and 3; do not affix border firmly at first corner until final border strip is applied. Roll outer edges of border and seams after 1/2 hour.

5

6

# More ideas for wallcovering panels

ABOVE: CEILING PANEL draws the eye upward. The placement lines for the panel were determined by measuring in 6″ (15 cm) from each wall.

OPPOSITE: WALL PANEL creates a border around a painting. Companion corner pieces are used for additional interest.

RIGHT: GROUPING OF PANELS adds interest to a wall. The square panels near the base of the wall are centered under a long horizontal panel.

# *W*allcovering Cutouts

Wallcovering cutouts are design motifs that are cut from wallcovering or borders. The cutout designs can be used to create interesting patterns or trompe l'oeil effects on painted walls. Unique designs can be created by combining motifs from different wallcoverings. For best results, walls should be painted with a high-grade washable paint, such as a low-luster or satin-sheen paint or a flat enamel.

For most wall applications, a clear vinyl adhesive will bond cutouts to the wall surface. If you are applying a border adhesive to prepasted cutouts, it may be desirable to remove the prepasted glue to reduce the thickness of the paper. Remove glue from prepasted wallcovering by soaking the cutout in water and lightly rubbing the pasted side. Blot the cutout with a towel to remove excess water; then apply the desired adhesive.

# How to apply a wallcovering cutout

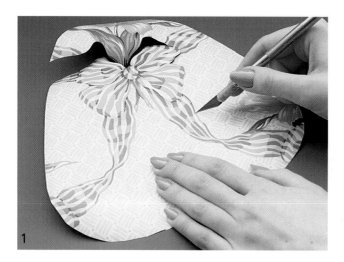

1. Cut wallcovering motifs using a mat knife and cutting surface or small, sharp scissors; simplify the designs as necessary. For easier handling, make any interior cuts before trimming outer edges.

2. Place the cutout facedown on a sheet of plastic or wax paper. Gently brush on a thin, even layer of adhesive, using a sponge applicator.

3. Press the cutout on surface; smooth out any air bubbles, using damp sponge. Roll the edges firmly with a seam roller. Rinse off any excess adhesive, using damp sponge.

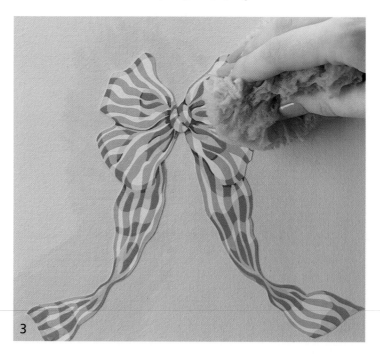

A

## TIPS FOR DECORATING WITH CUTOUTS

Create a focal point with pictures or plates by using design motifs like ribbons or ropes as faux hangers (A). Mark position of the picture or plate first, then cut the wallcovering motifs for positioning above and below. The motifs need not continue behind the object.

Extend length of a motif by cutting it apart and spreading the sections (B). Fill in the space between sections with smaller designs, such as flowers, rosettes, or bows.

Plan placement by positioning cutouts temporarily with poster putty (C). Mark the positions lightly with pencil or use positioned pieces as a guide when securing each motif in place.

B

C

# More ideas for wallcovering cutouts

OPPOSITE, TOP: TROMPE L'OEIL embellishes a kitchen wall. Plate, bowl, and vase motifs are cut from a wallcovering border and positioned above a shelf. Apple motifs and an edging strip, cut from a second border, help to unify the look.

OPPOSITE, BOTTOM: STORYBOOK SCENE is created by placing teddy bear motifs in the center of a wallcovering panel (page 25).

ABOVE: FLORAL ARCHWAY frames the upper portion of a window, for a feminine look.

RIGHT: HEADBOARD EFFECT is created by positioning cutouts on the wall above the bed.

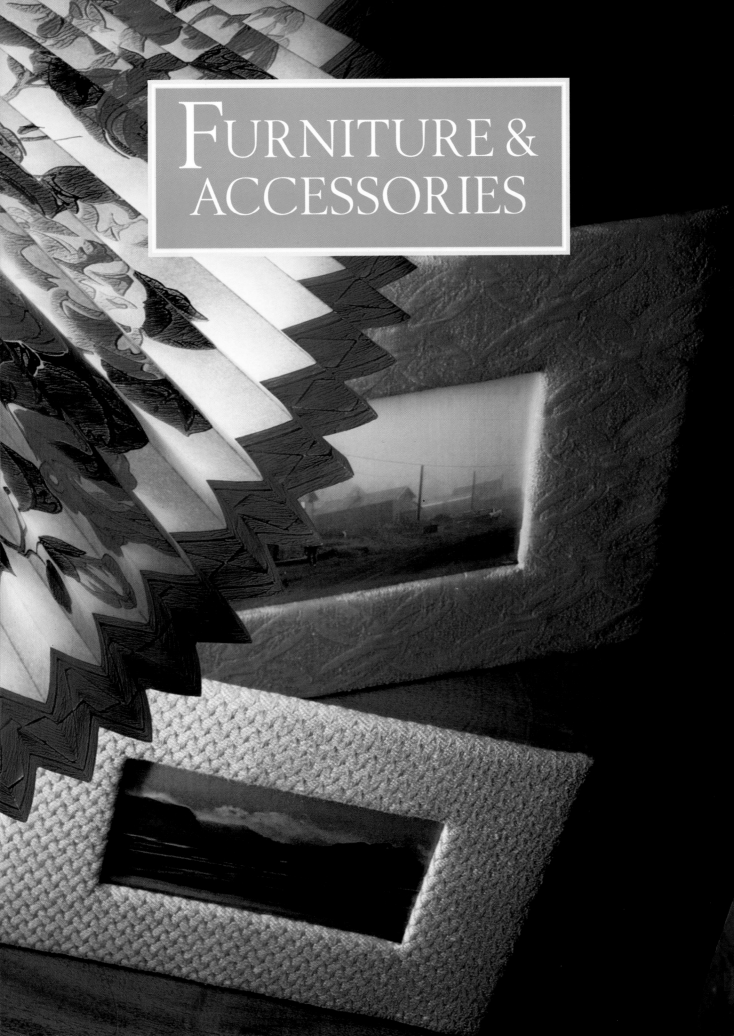

# FURNITURE & ACCESSORIES

# *W*allcovering on Furniture

Embellish tables and the flat surfaces of other furniture, such as trunks, dressers, and cabinets, with wallcovering to create distinctive furniture and accent pieces. For a quick embellishment, apply borders or cutouts. For a more intricate look, create your own custom design to imitate the look of tile or inlay. For this look, the wallcovering pieces are separated by narrow sections painted to simulate grout or spacers.

Tile or inlay designs can be as simple as cutting one wallcovering into squares or using several wallcoverings and more intricate pieces to create complex designs. Inlay designs are especially attractive when made from wallcoverings that imitate marble or stone. The paint chosen to imitate grout lines or spacers must be compatible with the surface being painted.

Wallcovering can be applied to most furniture surfaces, including metal, varnished, painted, and laminate. Apply the wallcovering using a border adhesive; this adhesive is suitable for all surfaces and ensures a strong bond.

To protect the wallcovering and to seal the edges, apply several coats of a clear finish, such as water-based polyurethane or acrylic finish, to the embellished surface. This finish can be applied over most surfaces and is easy to work with. For durability, select a finish that is recommended for surfaces that receive heavy use.

LEFT: INLAY DESIGNS on the coffee table and end table are made by cutting three different wallcoverings into design shapes. Spacer lines separating the shapes are painted gold.

# How to apply wallcovering to furniture in a tiled or inlaid design

## MATERIALS

- ◆ Wallcovering.
- ◆ Ammonia, for cleaning furniture surfaces.
- ◆ Fine-grit sandpaper, for deglossing shiny surfaces.
- ◆ Sheet of paper; transfer paper.
- ◆ Paint, for simulated grout or spacer lines.
- ◆ 1/4" (6 mm) tape, for marking simulated grout or spacer lines.
- ◆ Painter's masking tape.
- ◆ Border adhesive.
- ◆ Sponge applicator; sponge; seam roller.
- ◆ Mat knife or rotary cutter and cutting surface.
- ◆ Clear finish, such as water-based polyurethane or acrylic.
- ◆ Permanent markers or colored pencils, in colors to match the furniture surface or the edges of wallcovering, optional.

1. Measure the dimensions of the furniture, and plan the design on graph paper. Cut sheet of paper to design size, and mark points where design lines intersect. Use 1/4" (6 mm) tape and straightedge to mark grout or spacer lines on paper. It may be helpful to fold the paper into equal sections before marking design.

2. Prepare furniture surface as on page 42, step 1. Tape off outer edge of the design on furniture with painter's masking tape. Transfer any complex designs using transfer paper; simple designs may be transferred using straightedge and pencil.

3. Label top side of each design piece. Cut paper pattern apart along edges of tape lines; discard 1/4" (6 mm) tape strips. Tape pattern pieces to wallcovering, top side up; cut design pieces. The white cut edges of the wallcovering may be colored, using permanent marker or colored pencil that matches the furniture surface or wallcovering.

4. Paint over marked lines, applying paint wider than the 1/4" (6 mm) needed for grout or spacers; wallcovering pieces will partially cover the paint, leaving 1/4" (6 mm) between the pieces.

5. Position the wallcovering designs on the furniture surface; lightly mark placement lines. Complete the project as on page 42, steps 4 and 5; if the wallcovering expands after the adhesive is applied, trim pieces to size, using a mat knife.

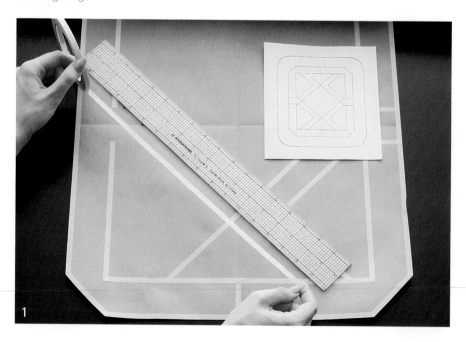

2

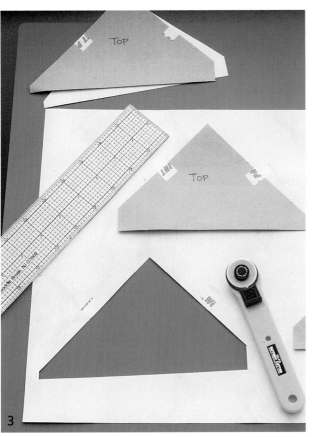

3

4

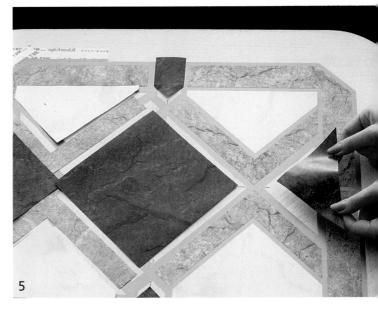

5

# How to apply wallcovering border & cutouts to furniture

## MATERIALS

- Wallcovering border and cutouts as desired.
- Ammonia, for cleaning furniture surfaces.
- Fine-grit sandpaper, for deglossing shiny surfaces.
- Border adhesive.
- Sponge applicator.
- Sponge.
- Seam roller.
- Mat knife and cutting surface, or small sharp scissors.
- Clear finish, such as water-based polyurethane or acrylic.
- Permanent markers or colored pencils, in colors to match the furniture surface or the edges of wallcovering, optional.

1. Clean furniture surface, using a solution of equal parts of ammonia and water, to remove any grease or soil. Degloss areas of shiny surfaces that will be covered with wallcovering, by lightly sanding with fine-grit sandpaper. This improves adhesion for the adhesive and clear finish.

2. Cut design motifs from wallcovering. White cut edges of wallcovering may be colored, using a permanent marker or colored pencil that matches furniture surface or wallcovering.

3. Arrange the designs on the surface as desired; lightly mark the position, using a pencil.

4. Apply an even coat of border adhesive to the back side of the wallcovering, using a sponge applicator. Press the wallcovering on the furniture surface; smooth out any air bubbles, using a damp sponge. Cut any mitered borders as on page 18; immediately roll the edges and seams of the wallcovering firmly with a seam roller. Allow to dry thoroughly.

5. Apply clear finish to the embellished surface, using a sponge applicator and following the manufacturer's directions; allow to dry. Repeat to apply three or more coats.

1

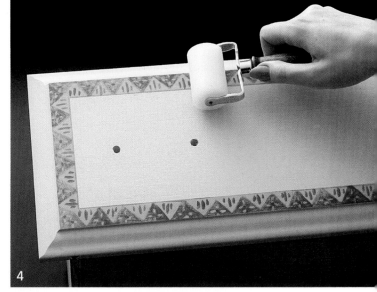

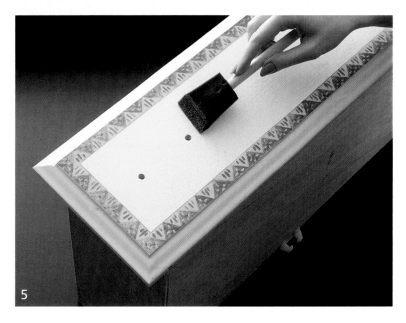

*More ideas
for wallcovering
on furniture*

LEFT: TABLE AND CHAIRS are embellished with wallcovering cutouts. Plate motifs cut from a border embellish the table. A floral motif cut from a different wallcovering decorates each chair back.

RIGHT: WALLCOVERING can be used to add design interest to ordinary furniture. A fruit basket wallcovering cutout creates a focal point on a desk. Wallcovering border edging strips outline the drawers and top of the desk.

BELOW: GAME TABLE is accented with wallcovering edged by a narrow rope border. Cards and chips were cut from a coordinating wallcovering.

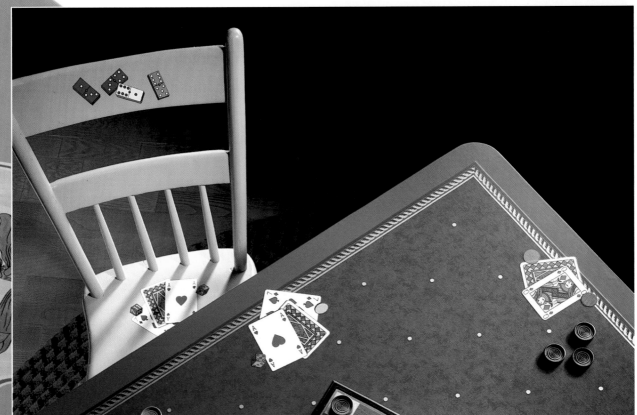

*Continued*

# *More ideas for wallcovering on furniture*
## (CONTINUED)

ABOVE: CHILDREN'S TOY CHEST is decorated with cars, trucks, and airplanes cut from a wallcovering border. Other wallcovering pieces are applied to the top and the lower edge of the chest.

OPPOSITE, TOP: CABINET has wallcovering applied to the inside of the door panels to create a trompe l'oeil effect.

OPPOSITE, BOTTOM: CHEST, painted with black paint, is embellished with Chinese-style motifs and border edging strips cut from wallcovering.

# Cornices

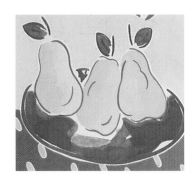

Use wallcovering borders to create sleek, tailored cornices. These cornices are especially attractive when used with simple undertreatments, such as shades, blinds, and sheer curtain panels. For a finished look, paint the edges of the cornice to match or coordinate with the edge of the wallcovering border.

Determine the inside measurements for the cornice only after any undertreatment is in place. The cornice should clear the undertreatment by 2″ to 3″ (5 to 7.5 cm), and it should extend at least 2″ (5 cm) beyond the end brackets for the rod on each side. Choose a wallcovering border that is wide enough for the completed cornice to cover any drapery heading and hardware.

## MATERIALS

- ¹/₂″ (3.8 cm) finish plywood with smooth finish on at least one side.
- Wallcovering border; border adhesive; sponge applicator.
- Wood glue; wood filler; medium-grit sandpaper.
- 16 × ¹/₂″ (3.8 cm) brads; nail set.
- Primer suitable for paint and wallcovering.
- Paint to coordinate with or match the edge of the wallcovering border.
- Angle irons; pan-head screws or molly bolts.

## CUTTING DIRECTIONS

Measure and cut the plywood for the top piece of the cornice to correspond to the inside measurements of the cornice, as necessary for the clearance of the undertreatment. Cut the cornice front piece to the expanded width of the wallcovering border (below). The cut width of the cornice front is equal to the width of the cornice top plus two times the thickness of the plywood. Cut the cornice side pieces equal to the expanded width of the wallcovering border by the depth of the cornice top.

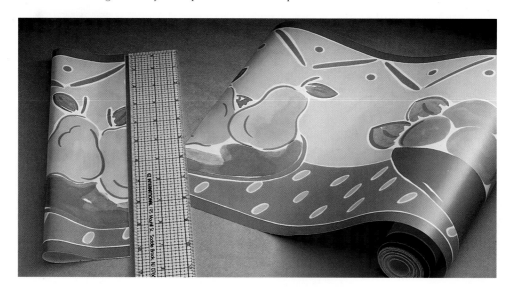

DETERMINE the expanded width of the wallcovering border by applying border adhesive to a 6" (15 cm) length of border. Fold the border in half; allow to set about 5 minutes, then remeasure the width. This is the actual height to cut the cornice front and side pieces.

# *How to make a cornice*

1. Glue and nail each side piece to the top piece, aligning the upper edges; secure with nails. Glue and nail the front piece, aligning it to the top and side pieces. Countersink nails. Fill the nail holes with wood filler; fill front, sides, and lower edges of plywood as necessary. Sand front and side surfaces and edges smooth.

**2.** Apply primer; allow to dry. Paint lower edges and top of the cornice, extending paint slightly over edges to front and sides; paint inside of cornice.

**3.** Cut wallcovering border equal to distance around the sides and front of the cornice plus 4″ (10 cm). Prepare wallcovering as for unpasted wallcovering (page 11), using border adhesive. Center wallcovering on cornice, wrapping wallcovering around the back edge of cornice just to the inside edge of plywood; trim excess paper.

**4.** Secure angle irons on inside of cornice top, near ends and at 45″ (115 cm) intervals or less. Hold cornice at desired placement, making sure it is level; mark the screw holes on wall or window frame. Remove angle irons from cornice. Secure angle irons to wall, using pan-head screws drilled into wall studs, or use molly bolts. Reattach the cornice to installed angle irons.

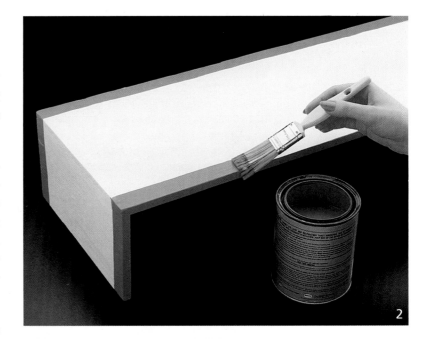

# More ideas for cornices

ABOVE: BORDER EDGING STRIP, cut from a companion wallcovering border, trims the upper and lower edges of a shaped cornice.

OPPOSITE, TOP: SCALLOPED BORDER is used to create a cornice with a shaped lower edge. The scallops are cut, using a jigsaw with a fine-toothed scroll-cut blade.

OPPOSITE, BOTTOM: STACKED BORDERS add height to this cornice.

# Lamp Shades

Make a customized lamp shade to coordinate with the decorating scheme of any room. Choose from either pleated or unpleated styles. Both versions use a purchased smooth lamp shade as a base.

For a pleated wallcovering shade, select a wallcovering or border that easily holds a crease, such as a paper-backed vinyl wallcovering. For an unpleated lamp shade from wallcovering, avoid using a wallcovering that has a striped or plaid pattern.

## How to make a pattern for an unpleated lamp shade

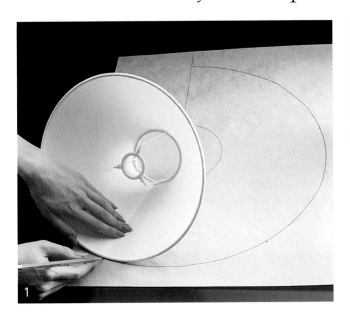

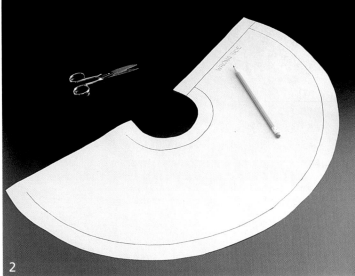

1. Mark a line, longer than the height of the lamp shade, on a large sheet of paper. Position lamp shade on paper, aligning seam of shade to the marked line. Roll lamp shade, and trace upper edge of shade to seam, using pencil; realign lamp shade seam with the marked line. Roll lamp shade, and trace lower edge of shade to seam.

2. Cut out paper pattern, allowing 1" (2.5 cm) excess paper around all edges. Label the pattern for wrong side of shade cover.

*Continued*

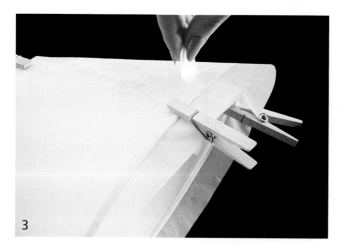

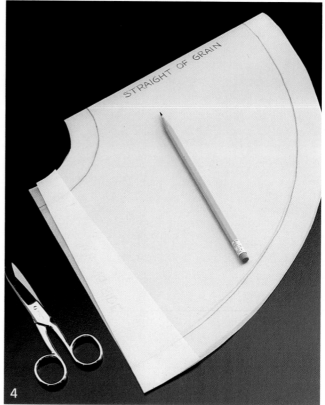

3. Position pattern on lamp shade, wrong side of pattern toward shade, aligning marked line to seam on shade; clamp, using clothespins. Tape ends together. Check fit of pattern, and redraw lines as necessary.

4. Remove the pattern; cut on straight line marked in step 1. Fold the pattern in half; crease. Mark crease for the lengthwise or crosswise direction of the wallcovering. Trim upper and lower edges of pattern, 5/8" (1.5 cm) from marked lines.

# How to make an unpleated wallcovering lamp shade

## MATERIALS

- Wallcovering.
- Smooth plastic or paper lamp shade, for base.
- Border adhesive; sponge applicator.
- Narrow trim, such as gimp or braid.
- Thick craft glue.
- Clothespins; sponge.

1. Make pattern (page 55). Position the pattern, wrong side down, on right side of wallcovering. Trace around pattern, adding 3/8" (1 cm) at one short end, for overlap. Cut on the lines marked on wallcovering.

2. Apply border adhesive to one-quarter of the lamp shade, starting about 3" (7.5 cm) from seam. Place cover on shade, aligning short end of cover with seam of shade; upper and lower edges will extend 5/8" (1.5 cm) beyond the edge of shade. Smooth out any air bubbles or wrinkles in the wallcovering. Continue to apply the wallcovering to the remainder of lamp shade, working with one-quarter section at a time; overlap the wallcovering at seam of shade. Remove any excess adhesive, using a damp sponge.

3. Continue to apply wallcovering to remainder of the lamp shade. Working with one-quarter section at a time, overlap wallcovering at seam of shade. Remove any excess adhesive, using damp sponge.

4. Make 1/2" (1.3 cm) clips, at 1/2" (1.3 cm) intervals, along upper edge of shade and at wire spokes. Fold wallcovering to inside of shade; secure, using border adhesive. Clamp the wallcovering in place as necessary with clothespins; allow to dry.

5. Make 1/2" (1.3 cm) clips, at 1/2" (1.3 cm) intervals, along lower edge of shade. Fold wallcovering to inside; secure with border adhesive, easing in extra fullness. Apply narrow trim to the upper and lower edges, to conceal edges of wallcovering; secure with thick craft glue.

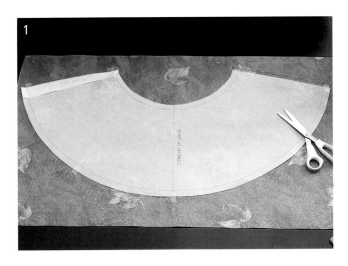

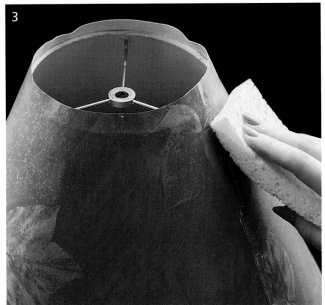

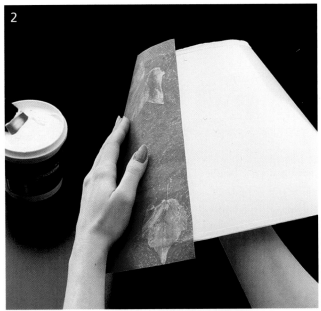

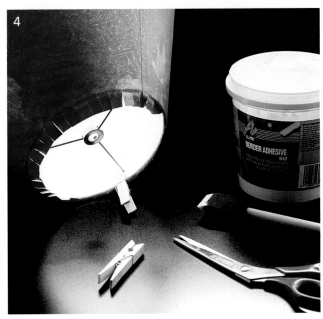

# How to make a pleated wallcovering lamp shade

## MATERIALS

- Wallcovering or wallcovering border, about ¾" (2 cm) taller than height of lamp shade.
- Smooth plastic or paper lamp shade, for base.
- Thick craft glue or hot glue gun and glue sticks.
- Transparent ruler.
- Soft elastic, about 1" (2.5 cm) wide, optional.
- String; plastic-coated paper clips.

1. Measure the height of the lamp shade along the sloped side; add ¾" (2 cm) to this measurement to determine cut width of the wallcovering. Measure the shade circumference at the lower edge; multiply by 2½ to determine the cut length of the wallcovering. Cut the wallcovering to these measurements.

2. Mark a light pencil line on the wrong side of the wallcovering, parallel to and 1" (2.5 cm) from the upper long edge of the strip. Repeat at the lower edge. Mark pleat lines within the marked lines, spaced 1½" (3.8 cm) apart and parallel to the short edges.

3. Fold the wallcovering on pleat lines, creasing sharply. Align adjacent pleat lines, and crease to fold crisp ¾" (2 cm) accordion pleats.

4. Overlap short ends of pleated wallcovering; trim excess wallcovering. Divide pleated wallcovering and shade into fourths at upper edges; mark, using paper clips.

5. Secure pleated wallcovering into tightly folded bundle, using string; cushion the bundle with narrow strips of wallcovering to prevent marking the wallcovering. Set aside for several hours to set pleats.

6. Overlap the short ends of the pleated wallcovering, and secure, using thick craft glue; allow to dry.

7. Position pleated wallcovering over lamp shade, matching marks. Adjust pleats so they are even and extend about ½" (1.3 cm) above shade. Elastic, cut to fit around upper and lower edges of shade, may help to control fullness while position of pleats is adjusted.

8. Secure pleated wallcovering to lamp shade at upper and lower edges, using thick craft glue or hot glue. Allow to dry.

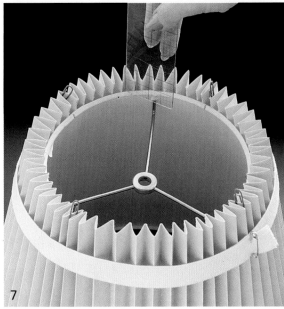

# *H*eadboards

Create a custom headboard by securing wallcovering to a wooden base, trimmed with corner molding. Additional decorative moldings can be added, if desired. The headboard is wall-mounted with sawtooth hangers, eliminating the need for attaching the headboard to the bed frame.

The width of the headboard is equal to the width of the bed frame plus an allowance for the bedding. The height of the headboard is about 20″ to 24″ (51 to 61 cm). A rectangular base is recommended for the headboard, for ease in mitering the corner molding. Make a paper pattern of the headboard, and place it on the wall behind the bed. Check the size and shape, and adjust as necessary. You may also want to locate the wall studs and mark their locations on the pattern.

When choosing wallcovering, select solid vinyls for the most durability; these will not absorb skin and hair oils. To avoid seams, select a wallcovering that can be applied horizontally.

# How to make a wallcovering headboard

## MATERIALS

- ¾" (2 cm) particleboard, cut to shape.
- Wallcovering and wallcovering border.
- Wallcovering primer; border adhesive.
- Wallcovering tools as needed (page 11).
- 1⅛" (2.8 cm) corner molding, for framing headboard.
- Decorative moldings, optional.
- ⅞" (2.2 cm) finishing nails; nail set.
- Miter box and backsaw.
- Paint, or stain and matching putty, for molding.
- Wood glue; fine-grit sandpaper.
- Large sawtooth picture hangers.
- Two 1½" × ¾" (3.8 × 2 cm) corner braces.

1. Apply wallcovering primer to particleboard; allow to dry. Paint or stain the back side of the particleboard, if desired.

2. Prepare the wallcovering as for unpasted wallcovering (page 11), using border adhesive. Apply wallcovering to particleboard, trimming edges even with edge of board. Position molding on upper edge of the headboard; mark inside edge of molding, using pencil. Repeat for sides. Prepare wallcovering border, and apply to upper edges and sides, lapping border ⅛" (3 mm) beyond marked lines; miter corners as on page 18.

3. Miter the corner molding for sides of headboard at upper corners, using backsaw and miter box; leave excess length on the molding strips. Miter one corner on moldings for upper and lower edges of headboard, leaving excess length.

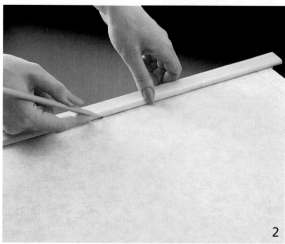

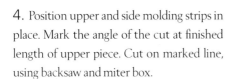

**4.** Position upper and side molding strips in place. Mark the angle of the cut at finished length of upper piece. Cut on marked line, using backsaw and miter box.

**5.** Reposition moldings. Mark finished length and angle of cut for each side piece; cut moldings on marked lines.

**6.** Position the lower molding, aligning mitered corner. Mark the finished length and angle of cut; cut miter. Reposition the moldings; sand the mitered corners, if necessary, for proper fit.

**7.** Paint or stain moldings as desired. Apply bead of glue to the molding, and position on the headboard. Use glue to secure mitered ends of moldings. Secure moldings to headboard, using finishing nails; predrill nail holes with 1/16" drill bit.

*Continued*

# How to make a wallcovering headboard
## (CONTINUED)

8. Countersink finishing nails, using nail set. Fill the holes with putty to match the stain, or touch up with paint.

9. Secure two to four sawtooth hangers to the back of the headboard, slotted edge down; position to align with wall stud locations, if possible.

10. Secure corner braces to lower edge of headboard, positioning one near each end. Hang headboard on wall, using sawtooth hangers. Secure corner braces to wall. Use molly bolts, if hangers and corner braces do not align with wall studs.

8

9

10

# More ideas for headboards

RIGHT: WALLCOVERING CUTOUTS are used as accents on a wallcovering headboard. Apply the cutouts as on pages 32 and 33.

BELOW: WALLCOVERING BORDER is used horizontally at the upper edge of a headboard. Decorative painted finials are secured on each end of the headboard. Predrill the holes for the finials through the corner molding and particleboard.

# Painting Styles

A cozy ambience seems to exist in a room when the walls have a textured appearance. This visual texture is easy and inexpensive to create with a variety of techniques, using water-based paints and glazes. Distinctive patterns can be created with strié or combing techniques, or an overall texture can be developed by rag rolling. Many common household materials can also be used to apply or partially remove paint glaze for unique texturized effects on walls, furniture, and accessories.

Sponge painting, in a choice of styles, can also enhance a painted surface. For a softly pebbled effect, paints are applied and blended, using sea sponges. Using cellulose sponges, a uniform repeating imprint can be made.

As another alternative, color washing can be used to create a soft, translucent effect on painted surfaces or wood. Color-washed walls have a subtle texture and shading, suitable for any decorating style. Used on wood, color washing creates a soft, translucent color that allows the natural tone and grain of the wood to show through.

These techniques and ideas will help you decorate your home with a creative touch. Easy-to-follow instructions with full-color photography help you learn these techniques quickly for results you'll be proud of.

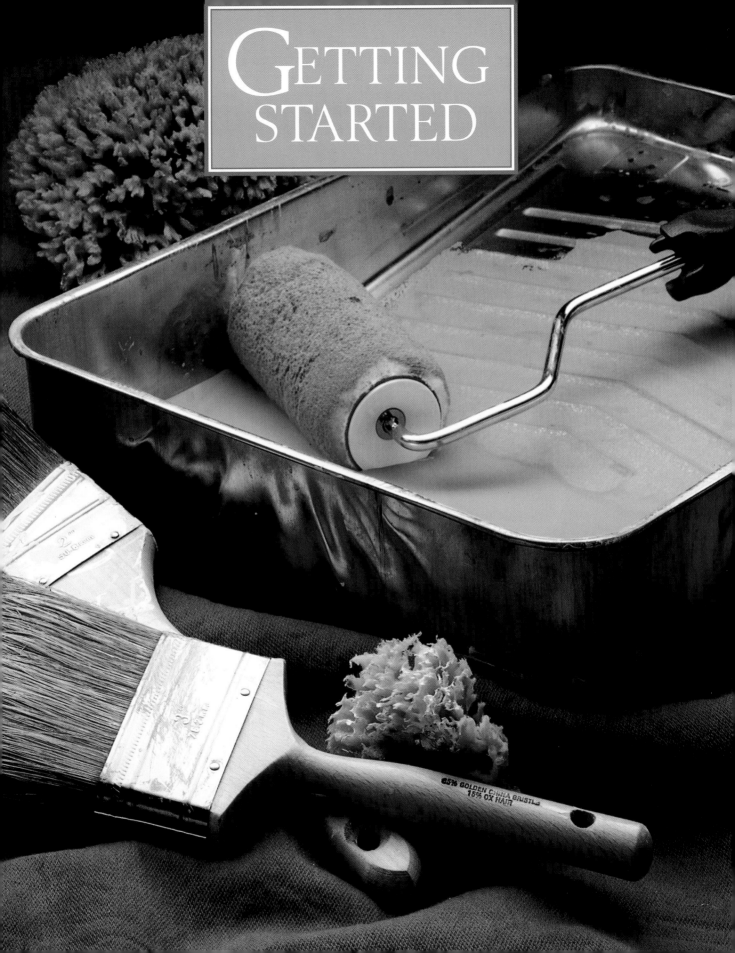

# GETTING STARTED

# Primers & Finishes

## PRIMERS

Some surfaces must be coated with a primer before the paint is applied. Primers ensure good adhesion of paint and are used to seal porous surfaces so paint will spread smoothly without soaking in. It is usually not necessary to prime a nonporous surface in good condition, such as smooth, unchipped, previously painted wood or wallboard. Many types of water-based primers are available; select one that is suitable for the type of surface you are painting.

A. FLAT LATEX PRIMER is used for sealing unfinished wallboard. It makes the surface nonporous so fewer coats of paint are needed. This primer may also be used to seal previously painted wallboard before you apply new paint of a dramatically different color. The primer prevents the original color from showing through.

B. LATEX ENAMEL UNDERCOAT is used for priming most raw woods or woods that have been previously painted or stained. A wood primer closes the pores of the wood, for a smooth surface. It is not used for cedar, redwood, or plywoods that contain water-soluble dyes, because the dyes would bleed through the primer.

C. RUST-INHIBITING LATEX METAL PRIMER helps paint adhere to metal. Once a rust-inhibiting primer is applied, water-based paint may be used on metal without causing the surface to rust.

D. POLYVINYL ACRYLIC PRIMER, or PVA, is used to seal the porous surface of plaster and unglazed pottery, if a smooth paint finish is desired. To preserve the texture of plaster or unglazed pottery, apply the paint directly to the surface without using a primer.

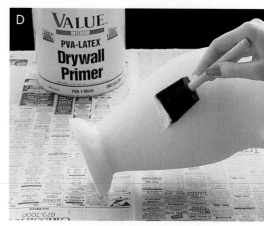

E. STAIN-KILLING PRIMER seals stains like crayon, ink, and grease so they will not bleed through the top coat of paint. It is used to seal knotholes and is the recommended primer for cedar, redwood, and plywood with water-soluble dyes. This versatile primer is also used for glossy surfaces like glazed pottery and ceramic, making it unnecessary to sand or degloss the surface.

## FINISHES

Finishes are sometimes used over paint as the final coat. They protect the painted surface with a transparent coating. The degree of protection and durability varies, from a light application of matte aerosol sealer to a glossy layer of clear finish.

F. CLEAR FINISH, such as water-based urethanes and acrylics, may be used over painted finishes for added durability. Available in matte, satin, and gloss, these clear finishes are applied with a brush or sponge applicator. Environmentally safe clear finishes are available in pints, quarts, and gallons (0.5, 0.9, and 3.8 L) at paint supply stores and in 4-oz. and 8-oz. (119 and 237 mL) bottles or jars at craft stores.

G. AEROSOL CLEAR ACRYLIC SEALER, available in matte or gloss, may be used as the final coat over paint as a protective finish. A gloss sealer also adds sheen and depth to the painted finish for a more polished look. Apply aerosol sealer in several light coats rather than one heavy coat, to avoid dripping or puddling. To protect the environment, select an aerosol sealer that does not contain harmful propellants. Use all sealers in a well-ventilated area.

# Tools & Supplies

## TAPES

When painting, use tape to mask off any surrounding areas. Several brands are available, varying in the amount of tack, how well they release from the surface without damaging the base coat, and how long they can remain in place before removal. You may want to test the tape before applying it to the entire project. The edge of the tape should be sealed tightly to prevent seepage.

## PAINT ROLLERS

Paint rollers are used to paint an area quickly with an even coat of paint. Roller pads, available in several nap thicknesses, are used in conjunction with roller frames. Use synthetic or lamb's wool roller pads to apply water-based paints.

A. SHORT-NAP ROLLER PADS with 1/4" to 3/8" (6 mm to 1 cm) nap are used for applying glossy paints to smooth surfaces like wallboard, wood, and smooth plaster.

B. MEDIUM-NAP ROLLER PADS with 1/2" to 3/4" (1.3 to 2 cm) nap are used as all-purpose pads. They give flat surfaces a slight texture.

C. LONG-NAP ROLLER PADS with 1" to 1 1/4" (2.5 to 3.2 cm) nap are used to cover textured areas in fewer passes.

D. ROLLER FRAME is the metal arm and handle that holds the roller pad in place. A wire cage supports the pad in the middle. Select a roller frame with nylon bearings so it will roll smoothly and a threaded end on the handle so you can attach an extension pole.

E. EXTENSION POLE has a threaded end that screws into the handle of a roller frame. Use an extension pole when painting ceilings, high wall areas, and floors.

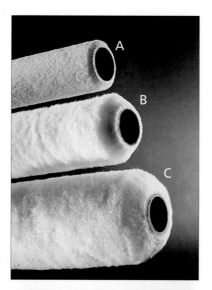

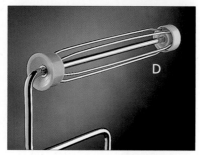

# PAINTBRUSHES & APPLICATORS

Several types of paintbrushes and applicators are available, designed for various purposes. Select the correct one to achieve the best quality in the paint finish.

A. SYNTHETIC-BRISTLE paintbrushes are generally used with water-based latex and acrylic paints, while B. NATURAL-BRISTLE brushes are used with alkyd, or oil-based paints. Natural-bristle paintbrushes may be used with water-based paints to create certain decorative effects.

C. BRUSH COMBS remove dried or stubborn paint particles from paintbrushes and align the bristles so they dry properly. To use a brush comb, hold the brush in a stream of water as you pull the comb several times through the bristles from the base to the tips. Use mild soap on the brush, if necessary, and rinse well. The curved side of the tool can be used to remove paint from the roller pad.

Stencil brushes are available in a range of sizes. Use the small brushes for fine detail work in small stencil openings, and the large brushes for larger openings. Either D. SNYTHETIC or E. NATURAL-BRISTLE stencil brushes may be used with acrylic paints.

Artist's brushes are available in several types, including F. FAN, G. LINER, and H. FLAT BRUSHES. After cleaning the brushes, always reshape the head of the brush by stroking the bristles with your fingers. Store artist's brushes upright on their handles or lying flat so there is no pressure on the bristles.

I. SPONGE APPLICATORS are used for a smooth application of paint on flat surfaces.

J. PAINT EDGERS with guide wheels are used to apply paint next to moldings, ceilings, and corners. The guide wheels can be adjusted for proper alignment of the paint pad.

# Preparing the Surface

To achieve a high-quality and long-lasting paint finish that adheres well to the surface, it is important to prepare the surface properly so it is clean and smooth. The preparation steps vary, depending on the type of surface you are painting. Often it is necessary to apply a primer to the surface before painting it. For more information about primers, refer to pages 70 and 71.

## PREPARING SURFACES FOR PAINTING

| SURFACE TO BE PAINTED | PREPARATION STEPS | PRIMER |
|---|---|---|
| UNFINISHED WOOD | 1. Sand surface to smooth it.<br>2. Wipe with damp cloth to remove grit.<br>3. Apply primer. | Latex enamel undercoat. |
| PREVIOUSLY PAINTED WOOD | 1. Clean surface to remove any grease and dirt.<br>2. Rinse with clear water; allow to dry.<br>3. Sand surface lightly to degloss and smooth it and to remove any loose paint chips.<br>4. Wipe with damp cloth to remove grit.<br>5. Apply primer to any areas of bare wood. | Not necessary, except to touch up areas of bare wood; then use latex enamel undercoat. |
| PREVIOUSLY VARNISHED WOOD | 1. Clean surface to remove any grease and dirt.<br>2. Rinse with clear water; allow to dry.<br>3. Sand surface to degloss it.<br>4. Wipe with damp cloth to remove grit.<br>5. Apply primer. | Latex enamel undercoat. |
| UNFINSHED WALLBOARD | 1. Dust with hand broom, or vacuum with soft brush attachment.<br>2. Apply primer. | Flat latex primer. |
| PREVIOUSLY PAINTED WALLBOARD | 1. Clean surface to remove any grease and dirt.<br>2. Rinse with clear water; allow to dry.<br>3. Apply primer, only if making a dramatic color change. | Not necessary, except when painting over dark or strong color; then use flat latex primer. |
| UNPAINTED PLASTER | 1. Sand any flat surfaces as necessary.<br>2. Dust with hand broom, or vacuum with soft brush attachment. | Polyvinyl acrylic primer. |
| PREVIOUSLY PAINTED PLASTER | 1. Clean surface to remove any grease and dirt.<br>2. Rinse with clear water; allow to dry thoroughly.<br>3. Fill any cracks with spackling compound.<br>4. Sand surface to degloss it. | Not necessary, except when painting over dark or strong color; then use polyvinyl acrylic primer. |
| UNGLAZED POTTERY | 1. Dust with brush, or vacuum with soft brush attachment.<br>2. Apply primer. | Polyvinyl acrylic primer or gesso. |
| GLAZED POTTERY, CERAMIC & GLASS | 1. Clean surface to remove any grease and dirt.<br>2. Rinse with clear water; allow to dry thoroughly.<br>3. Apply primer. | Stain-killing primer. |
| METAL | 1. Clean surface with vinegar or lacquer thinner to remove any grease and dirt.<br>2. Sand surface to degloss it and to remove any rust.<br>3. Wipe with damp cloth to remove grit.<br>4. Apply primer. | Rust-inhibiting latex metal primer. |
| FABRIC | 1. Prewash fabric without fabric softener to remove any sizing, if fabric is washable.<br>2. Press fabric as necessary. | None. |

# Water-based Paints

A wide variety of paint is available from paint supply stores and craft stores. Each type has advantages that make it especially suitable for certain kinds of painting. All of the following are water-based, making cleanup easy with soap and water. Water-based paints are also safer for the environment than oil-based paints.

## LATEX PAINTS

Latex paint is fast drying and durable. In addition to the wide range of premixed colors, latex paint can be custom-mixed by a paint professional. It is available in various finishes, from flat latex for a matte appearance to high-gloss latex with maximum sheen. Low-luster latex enamel paint, sometimes referred to as eggshell enamel, has some sheen and provides good coverage; semigloss has a bit more sheen. The glossier the paint, the more durable it is. Packaged in pints, quarts, and gallons (0.5, 0.9, and 3.8 L), latex paint is suitable for general use in small and large jobs.

Latex paint contains acrylic or vinyl resins or a combination of both. Latex paints of acrylic resins are the highest quality, with vinyl-acrylic blends next in quality, followed by paints consisting solely of vinyl resins. High-quality paints may cost significantly more, but they provide an even, complete coverage and wear longer.

## CRAFT ACRYLIC PAINT

Craft acrylic paint contains 100 percent acrylic resins. Generally sold in 2-oz., 4-oz., and 8-oz. (59, 119, and 237 mL) bottles or jars, these premixed acrylics have a creamy brushing consistency and give excellent coverage. They should not be confused with the thicker artist's acrylics used for canvas paintings. Craft acrylic paint can be diluted with water, acrylic extender, or latex paint conditioner (page 78) if a thinner consistency is desired. Craft acrylic paints are available in many colors and in metallic, fluorescent, and iridescent formulas.

## CERAMIC PAINTS

Ceramic paints provide a scratch-resistant and translucent finish. They can be heat-hardened in a low-temperature oven to improve their durability, adhesion, and water resistance. Latex and acrylic paints may also be used for painting ceramics, provided the surface is properly primed (page 75).

## FABRIC PAINTS

Fabric paints have been formulated specifically for painting on fabric. To prevent excessive stiffness in the painted fabric, avoid a heavy application; the texture of the fabric should show through the paint. Once the paints are heat-set with an iron, the fabric can be machine washed and dry-cleaned. Acrylic paints can also be used for fabric painting; textile medium may be added to the acrylics to make them more pliable on fabric.

# Paint Mediums

Paint mediums, such as conditioners, extenders, and thickeners, are often essential for successful results in decorative painting. Available in latex or acrylic, paint mediums are formulated to create certain effects or to change a paint's performance without affecting its color. Some mediums are added directly to the paint, while others are used simultaneously with paint. Mediums are especially useful for latex and acrylic paint glazes (page 83), in that they make an otherwise opaque paint somewhat translucent.

LATEX PAINT CONDITIONER, such as Floetrol®, was developed for use in a paint sprayer with latex paint, but this useful product is also essential in making paint glaze for faux finishes. When paint conditioner is added to paint, it increases the drying or "open" time and extends the wet-edge time to avoid the look of overlapping. The mixture has a lighter consistency and produces a translucent paint finish. Latex paint conditioner may be added directly to either latex or acrylic paint.

TEXTILE MEDIUM is formulated for use with acrylic paint, to make it more suitable for fabric painting. Mixed into the paint, it allows the paint to penetrate the natural fibers of cottons, wools, and blends, creating permanent, washable painted designs. After the fabric is painted, it is heat-set with an iron.

ACRYLIC PAINT EXTENDER thins the paint, increases the open time, and makes paint more translucent.

ACRYLIC PAINT THICKENER increases the drying time of the paint while it thickens the consistency. Thickener can be mixed directly into either acrylic or latex paint. Small bubbles may appear while mixing, but they will disappear as the paint mixture is applied. Thickener is used for painting techniques that require a paint with more body, such as combing.

# PAINTING WITH GLAZES

# *Paint Glaze Basics*

Many types of decorative painting require the use of a paint glaze, made by adding paint conditioner (page 78) or paint thickener (page 79) to the paint. With these paint mediums, the drying time of the paint is extended, allowing the additional time needed to manipulate the paint before it sets. The glaze has a creamy texture when wet and forms a translucent top coat once it dries.

Paint glazes have traditionally been made from oil-based paints. These oil glazes are messy to use, difficult to clean up, and noxious. Water-based latex and acrylic glazes, on the other hand, are easier to use, safer for the user and the environment, and lower in cost.

The basic glaze (below) is used for several types of decorative painting, including strié, combing, rag rolling, texturizing, and, sometimes, sponging. The glaze is varied slightly for color washing. Without the use of paint glazes, all of these finishes would be nearly impossible to achieve.

## TIPS FOR USING PAINT GLAZE

PROTECT the surrounding area with a drop cloth or plastic sheet and wear old clothing, because working with glaze can be messy.

USE wide painter's tape (page 72) to mask off the surrounding surfaces. Firmly rub the edges of the tape, to ensure that the glaze will not seep under it.

USE a paint roller to apply the glaze when even coverage is desired or when painting a large surface, such as a wall.

USE a paintbrush to apply the glaze when a paint finish with more variation and pattern in the surface is desired or when painting a small item.

USE a sponge applicator to apply the glaze when smooth coverage is desired or when painting a small item.

MANIPULATE the glaze while it is still wet. Although humidity affects the setting time, the glaze can usually be manipulated for a few minutes.

WORK with an assistant when using glaze on a large surface. While one person applies the glaze, the other can manipulate it.

## BASIC GLAZE

Mix together the following ingredients:

One part latex or craft acrylic paint in desired sheen.

One part latex paint conditioner, such as Floetrol®.

One part water.

# *How to apply a strié paint finish*

### MATERIALS

- Low-luster latex enamel in desired color, for the base coat.
- Latex paint in desired sheen and color, for the glaze.
- Latex paint conditioner, such as Floetrol®.
- Wide natural-bristle brush.
- Soft natural-bristle paintbrush.

1. Prepare the surface (page 75). Apply base coat of low-luster latex enamel; allow to dry. Mix the glaze (page 83); apply over base coat in a vertical section about 18" (46 cm) wide, using paint roller or natural-bristle paintbrush.

2. Drag a dry, wide natural-bristle paintbrush through wet glaze, immediately after glaze is applied; work from top to bottom in full, continuous brush strokes. To keep brush rigid, hold bristles of brush against surface with handle tilted slightly toward you. Repeat until desired effect is achieved.

3. Wipe the paintbrush occasionally on clean, dry rag to remove excess glaze, for a uniform strié look. Or rinse brush in clear water, and wipe dry.

4. Brush the surface lightly after the glaze has dried for about 5 minutes, if softer lines are desired; use a soft natural-bristle brush, and keep brush stokes in the same direction as streaks.

# Strié

Strié is a series of irregular streaks in a linear pattern, created by using a paint glaze. Especially suitable for walls, this painting technique can also be used for furniture pieces with flat surfaces.

For large surfaces, it is helpful to work with an assistant. After one person has applied the glaze, the other person brushes through the glaze before it dries, to achieve the strié effect. If you are working alone, limit yourself to smaller sections, if possible, since the glaze must be wet to create this look. If it is necessary to interrupt the process, stop only when a section is completed.

Because it can be messy to apply a strié finish, wear old clothing and protect the surrounding area with drop cloths and wide painter's tape. Firmly rub the edges of the tape, to ensure that the glaze will not seep under it.

Strié lends itself well to tone-on-tone colorations, such as ivory over white or tones of blue, although the color selection is not limited to this look. To become familiar with the technique and test the colors, first apply the finish to a sheet of cardboard, such as mat board.

# How to apply a combed paint finish

## MATERIALS

- Low-luster latex enamel paint in desired color, for base coat.

- Latex paint or craft acrylic paint in desired sheen and color, for glaze.

- Latex paint conditioner, for basic glaze; or acrylic paint thickener, for thickened glaze.

- Paintbrush, paint roller, or sponge applicator.

- Combing tool, opposite.

- Clear finish or aerosol clear acrylic sealer, optional.

1. Prepare the surface (page 75). Apply a base coat of low-luster latex enamel to surface, using a sponge applicator, paintbrush, or paint roller. Allow to dry.

2. Mix basic glaze (page 83) or thickened glaze (opposite); apply to small area at a time, using a sponge applicator, paintbrush, or paint roller. Drag combing tool through wet glaze to create pattern. Allow to dry. Apply clear finish or sealer, if desired.

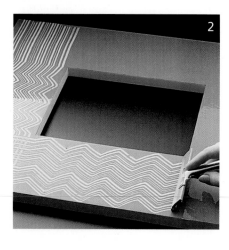

# Combing

Combing is a decorative painting technique that has been used for many years, as is evident by the number of antiques with this finish. For this technique, a paint glaze is applied over a base coat of paint. Narrow lines or stripes in the finish are created as you drag the teeth of a comb through the paint glaze, removing some of the glaze to reveal the base coat of paint. For a pronounced effect, the color of the paint glaze may contrast with that of the base coat.

A variety of combed patterns, such as wavy lines, scallops, crisscrosses, zigzags, and basket weaves, can be created. If you are unsatisfied with a particular pattern, the glaze can be wiped off while it is still wet, then reapplied; or the wet glaze can be smoothed out with a paintbrush, then combed into a different pattern.

You may use either the basic paint glaze (page 83) or a thickened glaze of two parts paint and one part acrylic paint thickener. The basic glaze produces a more translucent look and works well on walls and other surfaces without adding texture to the surface. The thickened glaze gives an opaque look with more distinct lines and texture.

A. RUBBER OR METAL COMBING TOOLS, available at craft and art stores, work well for this paint finish. If desired, you can make your own comb by cutting V grooves into a B. RUBBER SQUEEGEE or C. PIECE OF MAT BOARD.

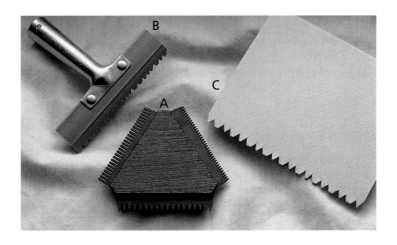

# Rag Rolling

Rag rolling is a painting technique that gives a rich, textural look with an allover mottled effect. It works well for walls and other flat surfaces, such as dresser tops and drawers, shelves, bookends, and doors. The basic paint glaze on page 83 can be used in either of the two techniques for rag rolling, *ragging-on* and *ragging-off.*

In ragging-on, a rag is saturated in the prepared paint glaze, wrung out, rolled up, and then rolled across a surface that has been base-coated with low-luster latex enamel paint. Rag-on a single application of glaze over the base coat, for a bold pattern. Or, for a more subtle, blended look, rag-on two or more applications of glaze.

In ragging-off, apply a coat of paint glaze over the base coat, using a paintbrush or paint roller; then roll up a rag and roll it over the wet glaze to remove some of the glaze. This process may be repeated for more blending, but you must work fast, because the glaze dries quickly.

If you are using the ragging-off method on large surfaces, such as walls, it is helpful to have an assistant. After one person applies the glaze, the second person can rag-off the area before the glaze dries. While it is not necessary to complete the entire room in one session, it is important that you complete an entire wall.

With either method, test the technique and the colors that you intend to use on a large piece of cardboard, such as mat board, before you start the project. Generally, a lighter color is used for the base coat, with a darker color for the glaze.

Feel free to experiment with the technique as you test it, perhaps rag rolling two different glaze colors over the base coat. Or try taping off an area, such as a border strip, and rag rolling a second or third color within the taped area.

Because the glaze can be messy to work with, apply a wide painter's tape around the area to be painted and use drop cloths to protect the surrounding surfaces. Wear old clothes and rubber gloves, and keep an old towel nearby to wipe your hands after you wring out the rags.

# How to apply a rag-rolled paint finish using the ragging-on method

## MATERIALS

- Low-luster latex enamel paint, for base coat.
- Latex or craft acrylic paint and latex paint conditioner, for glaze; 1 qt. (0.9 L) of each is sufficient for the walls of a 12 ft. x 14 ft. (3.7 x 4.33 m) room.
- Paint pail; rubber gloves; old towel; lint-free rags, about 24" (61 cm) square.

1. Prepare surface (page 75). Apply a base coat of low-luster latex enamel, using paint-brush or paint roller. Allow to dry.

2. Mix basic glaze (page 83) in pail. Dip lint-free rag into glaze, saturating entire rag; wring out well. Wipe excess glaze from hands with old towel.

3. Roll up the rag irregularly; then fold in half to a width equal to both hands.

4. Roll the rag over surface, working upward at varying angles. Rewet rag whenever necessary, and wring out.

5. Repeat the application, if more coverage is desired.

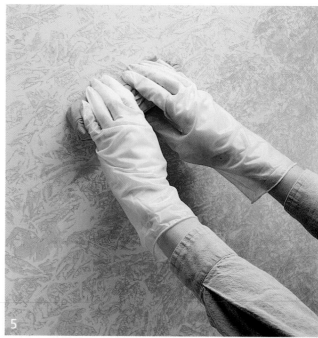

# *How to apply a rag-rolled paint finish using the ragging-off method*

1. Apply base coat of low-luster latex enamel, using paintbrush or paint roller. Allow to dry.

2. Mix basic glaze (page 83); pour into a paint tray. Apply the glaze over the base coat, using paint roller or paint pad.

3. Roll up lint-free rag irregularly; fold in half to width of both hands. Roll the rag through the wet glaze, working upward at varying angles.

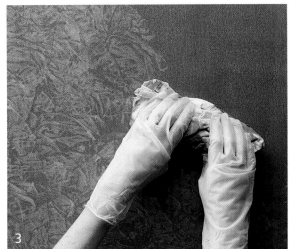

## COLOR EFFECTS

As shown in the examples below, the color of the base coat is not affected when the ragging-on method is used. With the ragging-off method, the color of the base coat is changed, because the glaze is applied over the entire surface, and then some glaze is removed with a rag to soften the background.

RAGGING-ON is used, applying aqua glaze over a white base coat. The white base coat remains unchanged.

RAGGING-OFF is used, applying aqua glaze over a white base coat. The white base coat is covered with the glaze, then appears as a lighter aqua background when some of the glaze is removed.

RAGGING-ON AND RAGGING-OFF are both used. First a taupe glaze is ragged-on over a white base coat. Then a rust glaze is ragged-off, changing the white base coat to a lighter shade of rust.

# Texturizing

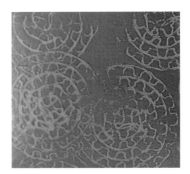

In addition to the methods for strié, combing, and rag rolling, numerous household items and painting supplies can be used with paint glaze to achieve finishes that have visual texture. Rolled or bent pieces of corrugated cardboard cheesecloth, crumpled paper, raffia, plastic wrap, carved potatoes, and scrub brushes create interesting textured effects. The list of items is as endless as your imagination.

For these finishes, use the basic glaze and instructions on page 83. You may apply a coat of glaze directly to the surface, then manipulate it or partially remove it by dabbing the glaze with the item or items you have selected. Or using the alternate method, the glaze may be applied to the selected items, then printed onto the surface. To become familiar with the methods and determine which effects you prefer, experiment with both methods, using a variety of items.

Apply a base coat of paint, using a good-quality low-luster latex enamel, before you apply the glaze. The base coat and the glaze may be in contrasting colors, such as emerald green over white. For a more subtle look, try a tone-on-tone effect, such as two shades of blue, or choose colors that are similar in intensity, such as deep red over deep purple. For even more possibilities, the process can be repeated, using one or more additional colors of glaze. This adds even more visual interest and is especially suitable for small accessories.

LEFT: ACCESSORIES have a variety of textural effects, created using folded cheesecloth for the vase, rolled corrugated cardboard for the bowl, and single-face corrugated cardboard for the tray.

## MATERIALS

- Low-luster latex enamel paint in desired color, for base coat.
- Latex or acrylic paint in desired sheen and color, for glaze.
- Latex paint conditioner, such as Floetrol®.
- Items selected for creating the textural effect.

# How to apply a texturized paint finish

1. Prepare surface (page 75). Apply a base coat of low-luster latex enamel, using sponge applicator, paintbrush, or paint roller. Allow to dry.

2. Mix glaze (page 83). Apply glaze to a small area at a time, using sponge applicator, paintbrush, or paint roller. A heavier coat of glaze gives a more opaque finish, and a light coat, a more translucent finish.

3. Texturize glaze by dabbing, rolling, or dragging items in the glaze to create patterns; rotate item, if desired, to vary the look. Replace the item as necessary, or wipe the excess glaze from item occasionally.

ALTERNATE METHOD. Follow step 1, above. Then apply glaze to selected item, using a sponge applicator, paintbrush, or paint roller; blot on paper towel or cardboard. Dab, roll, or drag glaze-covered item over base coat, to apply glaze to surface randomly or in desired pattern.

# Texturizing techniques

CARDBOARD. Rolled corrugated cardboard is secured by taping it together. Use corrugated end to make design in coat of wet glaze (A). Or apply glaze directly to cardboard; blot, and print designs on surface (B).

Single-face corrugated cardboard is cut to the desired shape. To make design, press corrugated side in coat of wet glaze (C). Or apply glaze directly to corrugated side; blot, and print designs on surface (D).

*Continued*

# Texturizing techniques

CHEESECLOTH. Fold cheesecloth into a flat pad and press into coat of wet glaze (A). Or apply glaze directly to a folded flat pad of cheesecloth, then imprint the cheesecloth onto the surface (B).

PAPER. Crumple paper and press into coat of wet glaze (C). Or apply glaze directly to paper; press onto the surface, crumpling the paper (D).

PLASTIC WRAP. Wrinkle plastic wrap slightly and place over coat of wet glaze; press lightly, and peel off (A). Or apply glaze directly to plastic wrap. Then place plastic wrap on the surface, folding and crinkling it; peel off (B).

FAN BRUSH. Press brush into wet glaze, making uniform rows of fan-shaped impressions (C). Or apply glaze directly to fan brush, and print fan-shaped designs on surface (D).

*Continued*

## *Texturizing techniques*

### (CONTINUED)

COARSE FABRIC. Fanfold a narrow length of burlap or other coarse fabric into a thick pad; apply glaze. Flip folds to back of pad as they become saturated, exposing fresh fabric for texturizing (A). Or, crumple a piece of coarse fabric into loose, irregular folds; apply glaze. Recrumple or start with a fresh piece as fabric becomes saturated (B).

TWINE OR STRING. To texturize with a distinctive pattern, use the twine or string as it comes in a ball. Apply glaze; press onto surface, turning ball or unwinding twine or string as areas become saturated (C). Or, wind string or twine erratically into a tangle for more irregularly shaped pattern (D). Apply glaze and press onto surface.

COARSE NETTING (A). Apply glaze to netting balls, such as those found in bath shops; press onto surface. Netting will not absorb the glaze, so will not become saturated.

SPATTERING (B). Protect the work surface with drop cloths. Mix paints in small cups, combining two parts paint with one part water. Dip tip of brush into paint; remove excess paint on edge of cup. Hold stick and brush over project; strike brush handle against stick to spatter paint. Work from top to bottom in wide strips. Allow first color of paint to dry. Repeat steps for each color, as desired.

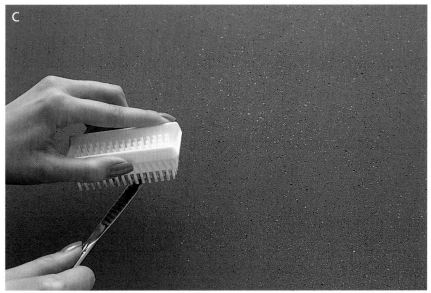

SPECKING (C). Dip ends of stiff-bristled brush into thinned paint. Tap brush onto piece of paper to remove excess paint. Hold brush over surface to be painted; flick bristles toward you using knife or finger, spraying paint away from you. The closer to the surface the brush is held, the finer the spattering and the more control you have.

# More ideas for painting with glazes

LEFT: GLAZE FINISHES (page 83) are combined to decorate this small jewelry box. The top and sides of the box are sponge painted; from top to bottom, the drawers are painted using the ragging-on, texturizing, and combing techniques.

CENTER: SPECIALTY PAINT ROLLER quickly creates visual texture on a fabric surface. The roller can be used on hard surfaces, as well.

RIGHT: COMBED SURFACE emphasizes the unique shape of this vase.

*Continued*

# More ideas for painting with glazes
(CONTINUED)

102

TOP: RAG ROLLING adds textural interest to walls, furniture, and accessories. This
tabletop was painted by ragging-off.

LEFT: MAGAZINE RACK is painted by
applying two colors of paint, using the ragging-
on method (page 90). A final coat of aerosol
clear acrylic sealer adds luster and provides a
durable finish.

OPPOSITE: VISUAL TEXTURE was applied
to this wall, using crumpled burlap.

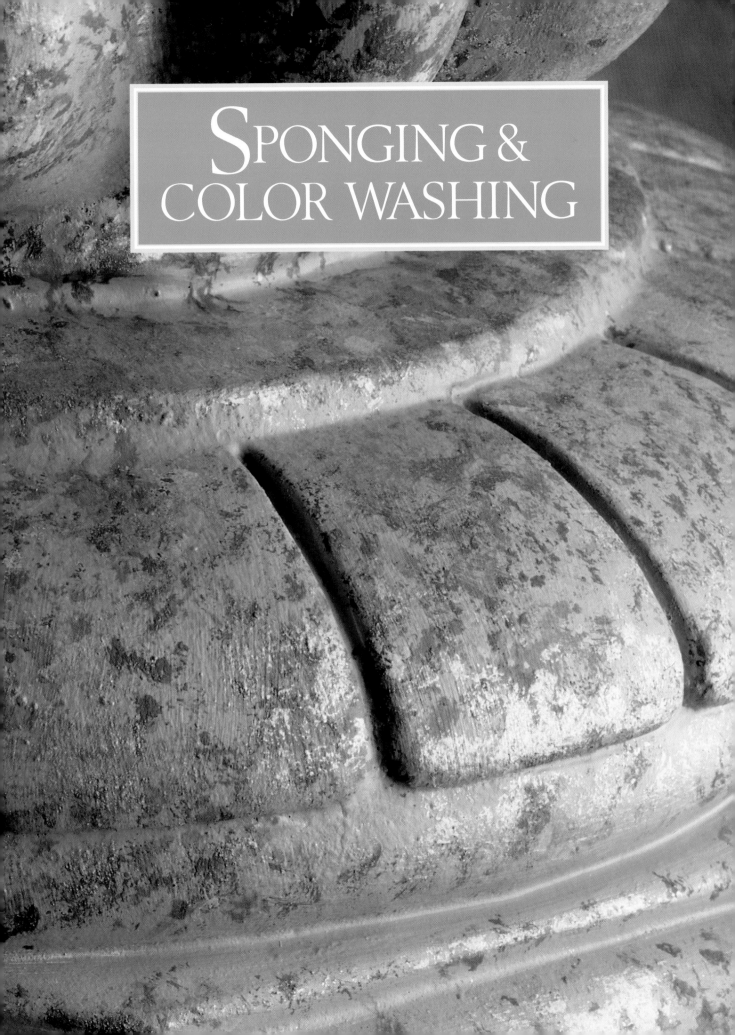

# SPONGING &
# COLOR WASHING

# *S*ponge Painting

Sponge painting produces a soft, mottled effect and is one of the easiest techniques to use. To achieve this paint finish, use a natural sea sponge to dab paint onto a surface. Cellulose or synthetic sponges should not be used because they tend to leave identical impressions with hard, defined edges.

The sponged look can be varied, depending on the number of paint colors applied, the sequence in which you apply the colors, and the distance between the sponge impressions. You can use semigloss, low-luster, or flat latex paint for the base coat and the sponging. Or for a translucent finish, use a paint glaze that consists of paint, paint conditioner, and water; make the glaze as on page 83.

To create stripes, borders, or panels, use painter's masking tape to mask off the desired areas of the surface after the first color of sponged paint is applied. Then apply another color to the unmasked areas.

Fabric may be sponge painted, using fabric paint (page 77) or craft acrylic paint mixed with textile medium (page 79). Prewash fabric to remove any sizing, if fabric is washable, and press well to remove wrinkles. Apply paint with sea sponge, as in step 2 on page 108, but do not blot with a wet sponge. When the fabric is dry, heat-set the paint using a dry iron and a press cloth.

# How to sponge paint

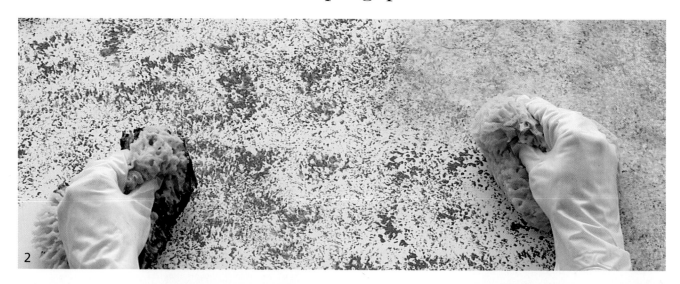

## MATERIALS

- Craft acrylic or latex paints in desired sheens and colors, for base coat and for sponging.
- Natural sea sponge.
- Painter's masking tape.
- Carpenter's level, for painting stripes, borders, or panels.

1. Prepare surface (page 75). Apply base coat of desired color. Allow to dry. Rinse sea sponge in water to soften it; squeeze out most of the water. Saturate sponge with paint or with paint glaze (page 83). Blot the sponge lightly on paper towel.

2. Press sponge repeatedly onto surface, as shown at left; work quickly in small areas, and change position of sponge often. Blot paint on surface immediately, using wet sea sponge in other hand, as shown at right; this causes the paint to bleed, for a softened, blended look. Some of the paint is removed with the wet sponge.

3. Continue to apply the first paint color to entire project, blotting with moist sponge. Repeat steps with one or more additional colors of paint, if desired. Allow paint to dry between colors.

4. Optional feathering. Apply final color of paint, using a light, sweeping motion instead of dabbing.

# How to sponge paint stripes, borders, or panels

1 Follow steps 1 to 3, opposite. Allow paint to dry thoroughly. Mark light plumb line, using a pencil and carpenter's level. Position first row of painter's masking tape along this line.

2. Measure and position remaining rows of painter's masking tape to mark stripes, borders, or panel areas.

3. Apply second paint color to the unmasked areas of the surface. Allow paint to dry.

4. Remove the painter's masking tape, revealing two variations of sponge painting.

## COLOR EFFECTS

When related colors are used for sponge painting, such as two warm colors or two cool colors, a harmonious look is achieved. For a bolder and more unexpected look, sponge paint in a combination of warm and cool colors.

WARM COLORS like yellow and orange blend together for an exciting effect.

COOL COLORS like green and blue blend together for a tranquil effect.

WARM AND COOL COLORS like yellow and blue combine boldly, but sponge painting softens the effect.

# Sponge Painting a Check Design

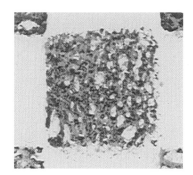

For a dramatic check pattern on walls, apply paint with squares of cellulose sponge. For easier application of the paint, glue the sponge to a piece of plywood and use it as a stamp. As a final step, add more dimension and color to the design, if desired, by lightly stamping another paint color over the checks. For this second paint color, use a square stamp of the same size, or make a stamp in a smaller size or shape.

For even rows, the check pattern works best for walls that have squared corners and ceiling lines. A plumb line may be used as a vertical guide. Plan to start painting at the most prominent corner of the room and work in both directions so full squares will meet at that corner. You may want to divide the dominant wall evenly into checks across the width of the wall.

Flat latex or low-luster latex enamel paint may be used for painting walls. To provide a more durable finish on cabinets and furniture, use a gloss enamel.

# *How to sponge paint a check design*

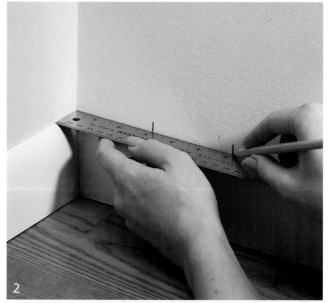

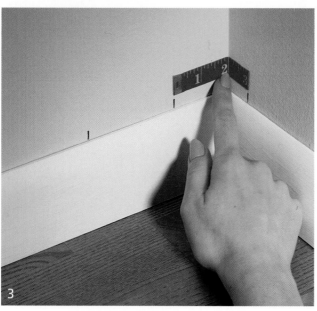

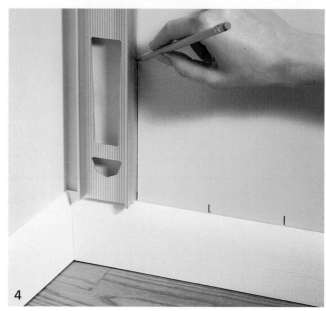

## MATERIALS

- Latex paint in desired background color, for base coat.
- Latex paint in one or more colors, for stamped design.
- Large cellulose sponges.
- Scraps of 1/4" (6 mm) plywood; hot glue gun and glue sticks.
- Thin transparent Mylar® sheets.

1. Cut cellulose sponge into the desired size of square for check design; cut plywood to same size. Make a stamp by securing sponge to plywood, using hot glue. Make one stamp for each color and shape in design.

2. Prepare surface (page 75). Apply base coat of paint in desired background color; allow to dry. Mark placement for first row of design, at bottom of wall, using pencil. For example, for a 3" (7.5 cm) stamp, lightly mark wall at 3" (7.5 cm) intervals. (Pencil markings are exaggerated to show detail.)

3. Mark the wall to corner. If full width of the design does not fit into the corner, measure around corner, and mark. Then continue marking full widths. Mark spaces on all walls.

4. Lightly mark a plumb line on wall, at the first marking from corner, using a level and pencil. Or hang a string at corner, using a pushpin near top of wall; weight string at bottom so it acts as a plumb line.

5. Apply paint to the sponge, using paint-brush. Stamp the bottom row of checks onto the wall.

6. Continue to stamp rows of checks, working up from bottom of wall and using previous row and plumb line as horizontal and vertical guides. If full stamped design does not fit into corners or at top of wall, leave area unpainted at this time.

7. Allow paint to dry. To fill in areas with partial stamped designs, place a piece of Mylar over previously painted checks to protect wall. Stamp design up to corners and top of wall, overlapping stamp onto Mylar. Allow paint to dry.

8. Add dimension and color to check design, if desired, using stamp of same size and shape as checks, or cut to a different size and shape. Apply another paint color, stamping very lightly over painted checks. Dispose of used stamps.

# *More ideas for sponge painting*

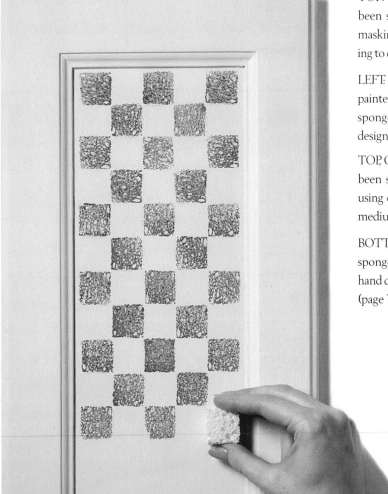

TOP: FLANGED PILLOW SHAMS have been sponged, using textile paints. Apply masking tape inside the border while sponging to define the edges of the flange.

LEFT: CHECKED CABINET DOORS are painted, using small sponges as stamps. The sponges were cut to size so the finished design fits within the door panel.

TOP, OPPOSITE: CURTAIN FABRIC has been sponge painted in a striped pattern, using craft acrylic paint mixed with textile medium (page 79).

BOTTOM, OPPOSITE: CERAMICS are sponge painted and decorated with free-hand designs, using specialty ceramic paints (page 77).

# Color-washed Walls

Color washing is an easy paint finish that gives walls a translucent, watercolored look. It adds visual texture to flat drywall surfaces, and it further emphasizes the already textured surface of a plaster or stucco wall.

In this technique, a color-washing glaze is applied in a cross-hatching fashion over a base coat of low-luster latex enamel, using a natural-bristle paintbrush. As the glaze begins to dry, it can be softened further by brushing the surface with a dry natural-bristle paintbrush. Complete one wall before moving on to the next or before stopping. Store any remaining glaze in a reclosable container between painting sessions.

The color-washing glaze can be either lighter or darker than the base coat. For best results, use two colors that are closely related or consider using a neutral color like beige or white for either the base coat or the glaze. Because the glaze is messy to work with, cover the floor and furniture with drop cloths and apply painter's tape along the ceiling and moldings.

## COLOR-WASHING GLAZE

Mix together the following ingredients:

One part flat latex paint.

One part latex paint conditioner.

Two parts water.

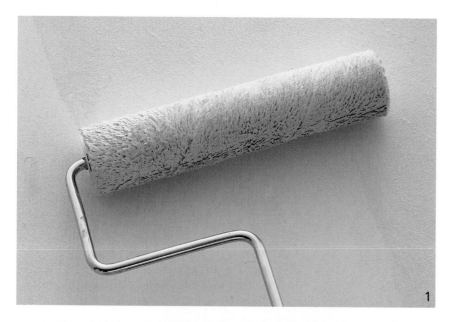

# How to
# color wash walls

## MATERIALS

- Low-luster latex enamel paint, for base coat.
- Flat latex paint, for color-washing glaze.
- Latex paint conditioner, for color-washing glaze.
- Paint roller.
- Two 3" to 4" (7.5 to 10 cm) natural-bristle paintbrushes for each person.
- Drop cloths; painter's tape.

1. Prepare the surface (page 75). Apply a base coat of low-luster latex enamel paint in the desired color, using a paint roller. Allow to dry.

2. Mix the color-washing glaze (page 117). Dip paintbrush into the glaze; remove excess glaze against rim of the container. Apply the glaze to wall in cross-hatching manner, beginning in one corner. The more you brush over the surface, the softer the appearance.

3. Brush over the surface, if desired, using a dry natural-bristle paintbrush, to soften the look. Wipe excess glaze from the brush as necessary.

A

B

## COLOR EFFECTS

Select colors for the base coat and the glaze that are closely related, or use at least one neutral color. A darker glaze over a lighter base coat gives a mottled effect. A lighter glaze over a darker base coat gives a chalky or watercolored effect.

Apply a darker top coat, such as a medium turquoise, over a lighter base coat, such as white (A).

Apply a lighter top coat, such as white, over a darker base coat, such as coral (B).

Apply two shades of a color, such as a medium blue top coat over a light blue base coat (C).

C

# Color-washed Finish
## for Wood

A subtle wash of color gives an appealing finish to wooden cabinets and accessories. This finish works for all decorating styles, from contemporary to country.

For color washing, a flat latex or acrylic paint is diluted with water. Applied over unfinished or stained wood, the color wash allows the natural wood tone and grain to show through. The lighter the original surface, the lighter the finished effect. To lighten a dark surface, first apply a white color wash, followed by a color wash in the desired finish color.

If you are applying a color wash to a varnished surface, remove any grease or dirt by washing the surface. It is important to roughen the varnish by sanding it, so the wood will accept the color-wash paint.

BELOW:   COLOR-WASHED STRIPES have been applied to a wooden charger for a cheerful country accent.

# How to apply a color-washed finish

## MATERIALS

- Flat latex paint.
- Matte or low-gloss clear acrylic sealer or finish.
- Paintbrush.
- 220-grit sandpaper.
- Tack cloth.

1. Prepare wood surface by cleaning and sanding it; if surface is varnished, roughen it with sandpaper. Wipe with damp cloth.

2. Mix one part flat latex paint to four parts water. Apply to wood surface, brushing in direction of wood grain and working in an area no larger than 1 sq. yd. (0.95 sq. m) at a time. Allow to dry for 5 to 10 minutes.

3. Wipe surface with clean, lint-free cloth to partially remove paint, until desired effect is achieved. If the color is too light, repeat the process. Allow to dry. Lightly sand surface with 220-grit sandpaper to soften the look; wipe with damp cloth.

4. Apply one to two coats of clear acrylic sealer or finish, sanding lightly between coats.

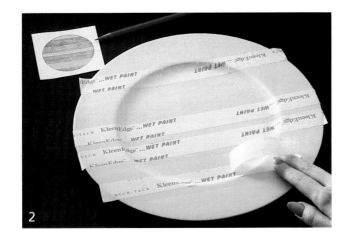

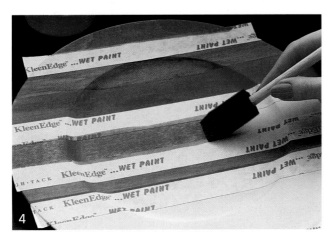

# How to apply color-washed stripes

## MATERIALS

- Craft acrylic paints in desired colors.
- 100-grit, 150-grit, and 220-grit sandpaper.
- Damp cloth.
- Painter's masking tape.
- Sponge applicator.
- Clear finish or aerosol clear acrylic sealer.

1. Sand the charger in the direction of the wood grain, using 150-grit sandpaper, then 220-grit sandpaper. Remove any grit, using a damp cloth.

2. Determine the desired color and width of each stripe in the charger, repeating colors as desired. Using painter's masking tape, mask off each side of stripes for the first paint color.

3. Dilute the paints, one part paint to two parts water. Apply the first paint color lightly to the masked stripes, using a sponge applicator; use paint sparingly. Allow to dry; remove tape.

4. Repeat steps 2 and 3 for each remaining paint color, allowing the paint to dry between colors.

5. Sand painted charger in the direction of wood grain, using 100-grit sandpaper, to give a worn appearance to the surface, especially sanding along outer and inner edges of the rim.

6. Apply a coat of clear finish or aerosol clear acrylic sealer to the charger. Apply additional coats as desired, sanding smooth between coats.

# *Index*